Materials
Teachers' notes

Aims of this book

This book provides photocopiable activities for children aged three to five to support the development of science concepts and skills. No special resources are needed, other than those usually to be found in nurseries or reception classes. The activities prepare for later learning in the National Curriculum/Scottish 5–14 guidelines. Children should be involved as much as possible in practical, hands-on activities.

Learning about materials

Children should have opportunities to explore and describe different materials. They should also consider what makes materials suitable for specific uses. The sheets will give a focus and act as a record of the children's practical experiences. NB Care should always be taken when handling resources. Young children may need support in activities which require cutting.

Notes on individual activities

Page 3: Made from plastic

Sorting and classifying need to be practised. Offer some children just the plastic materials needed, while others may have different materials. Plastic bottles should initially be cut up by an adult. Children may be able to cut smaller pieces for themselves, but cover sharp edges.

Page 4: Made from wood

Children should realise they are sorting things according to the material they are made from, not what they have been made into. Start to consider where wood comes from.

Page 5: Made from metal

Encourage the children to describe the materials as they sort. Discuss the materials used to make a car. Which parts are metal?

Page 6: Made from paper

Challenge the children to think of as many uses for paper as possible. A display of different types of paper is a good stimulus. Some children may like to make their own wrapping paper by printing with various objects.

Page 7: Sort out the cupboard

Children should stick one type of material/object in each compartment. What criteria have they used for sorting the objects?

Page 8: Magnetic materials

Children should understand that a magnet will pick up only some things. Allow time for play with the magnets first. If the objects are small and inexpensive, they can be stuck on to the sheet.

Page 9: Gone fishing

Use the fish as templates for making several sets of coloured fish. Mount on card and cover with sticky-backed plastic. Attach a paper-clip to the 'nose' of each fish. Make a fishing rod from a dowel and string, with a magnet on the end. Up to four children can play. Each child has a sheet to match the fish they catch. The first to match all the fish is the winner. Throw duplicates back in.

Page 10: Put them to bed

Children should begin to distinguish between different materials according to texture, colour, pattern. Ask them to select their own fabrics.

Page 11: The lighthouse

Discuss how a lighthouse works. What materials would be used for the various parts of the building? Select appropriate materials to cover the picture, such as shiny material for the sea.

Page 12: Keeping dry

To prepare, give the children a variety of materials (plastic sheeting, cotton fabric, paper, woollen material, lace) to choose from and test to find out if they are waterproof. Cut the top off a plastic soft drink bottle (cover any sharp edges with adhesive tape). Put a small plastic figure in the bottom and stretch a piece of material over the top, securing it with an elastic band. Pour a small amount of water on to the material to test.

Page 13: See through it

Cut the materials into pieces that will fit the window-panes. Children should sort the materials according to whether they are transparent or opaque. You can cut holes in the sheet first.

Page 14: Keeping warm

Encourage children to think about the insulating properties of materials. Provide a variety of materials to feel and talk about.

Page 15: Keeping cool

Children should be encouraged to think about and discuss times when we would want to keep cool. Include light (summer) materials in the selection of fabrics offered to the children.

▲ EARLY YEARS ESSENTIALS FOR SCIENCE: Materials

Page 16: The three little pigs
Read the story of the Three Little Pigs. Talk about the suitability of various materials for building houses. Go on to make 3D models.

Page 17: Squashy things
Give children a box containing samples of the materials, and allow them time to handle and discuss them. They can then complete the sheet.

Page 18: Does it float?
Children should know that some things will float while others sink. Experiment with the water tray first. Stick the small objects on to the sheet, or older children could draw them.

Page 19: Can you wiggle it?
Encourage the children to handle the materials and talk about them before selecting suitable ones to stick along the snakes. Compare materials such as ribbon and wool with lolly sticks.

Page 20: Play dough shapes
Children should be helped to understand that the shape of some materials can be changed by squashing, twisting, bending or stretching. What materials cannot be changed like this?

Page 21: Is it shiny?
Help children to distinguish between shiny and dull materials. They may need guidance to avoid sticking on to the handle and frame. Mount the mirror on card and cut out for the home corner.

Page 22: Make a snack mat
This activity helps children to appreciate the flexibility of paper. Prepare the sheets by cutting the slots (use a sharp knife or fold and cut with scissors). It may be easier to manage if one end of the paper strip to be woven is fixed with a spot of adhesive to the side of the sheet. The other end may be fixed when the mat is completed.

Page 23: Magic painting
This activity is meant to help children appreciate the water-repellent properties of wax. The picture must be coloured in quite thickly, and the paint be very thin, if the process is to work.

Page 24: Sticky stuff
Children should recognise the suitability of different materials for different purposes. The objects chosen need to be reasonably small. Use one copy of the sheet for each adhesive. Hold the paper up to see which materials have stuck.

Page 25: Melting
Prepare for this activity by placing ice-cubes in different locations and watch what happens to them. When the children have matched the pictures, discuss why the materials have changed. How might they be changed back?

Page 26: Lemonade
Add a spoonful of sherbet to the water in the glass and stir. Discuss where the powder has gone. Some children may find other materials that are soluble: salt, sugar, coffee. Make the silver bubbles from silver foil using a hole punch.

Page 27: Shades
Children should appreciate that they can change the shades of the colours they use by adding water (or white or black paint). Put a little coloured paint into a yoghurt pot, paint the first section using this paint and then gradually add more water to the pot, painting the next section after each time you add water.

Page 28: Blowing bubbles
Be aware of children with asthma or eczema who might suffer in this activity. Different-shaped blowers may be made from pipe-cleaners, but take care with the ends of the wires.

Page 29: Painting with soils
Collect soils from different localities, as far apart as possible, to show that not all soils are the same colour or texture. Use them as paint blocks, or mix to a mud. Make sure the children's clothes are well covered for this activity.

Page 30: Make a feely picture
Discuss and handle the materials to decide which are suitable. Use a PVA-type glue.

Page 31: Sorting muesli
Children need to understand that some things may be made from a mixture of other things, and that sometimes it is possible to separate them. Sieves with different-sized meshes may be used to separate mixtures of solid particles. Separating muesli enables children to find a wide variety of constituents in one mixture. Use sticky-backed plastic to attach a small amount of the contents of each sieve to the appropriate bowl.

Page 32: Texture dominoes
With adult help, the children can make their own domino set. Make the dominoes by sticking the appropriate materials on to each domino section, then mounting them on thick card and cutting them out along the dotted lines.

Up to four children can play. Encourage them to use the senses of touch and sight to play the game. The player with the 'double fur fabric' domino starts. The winner is the first player to get rid of all their dominoes. Play the game blindfold to make it more difficult.

▲ Name _____

Made from plastic

You will need: a collection of plastic materials (bottle tops, plastic bottles, carrier bags and so on) cut into small pieces, glue, scissors.

Use the materials to decorate each object.

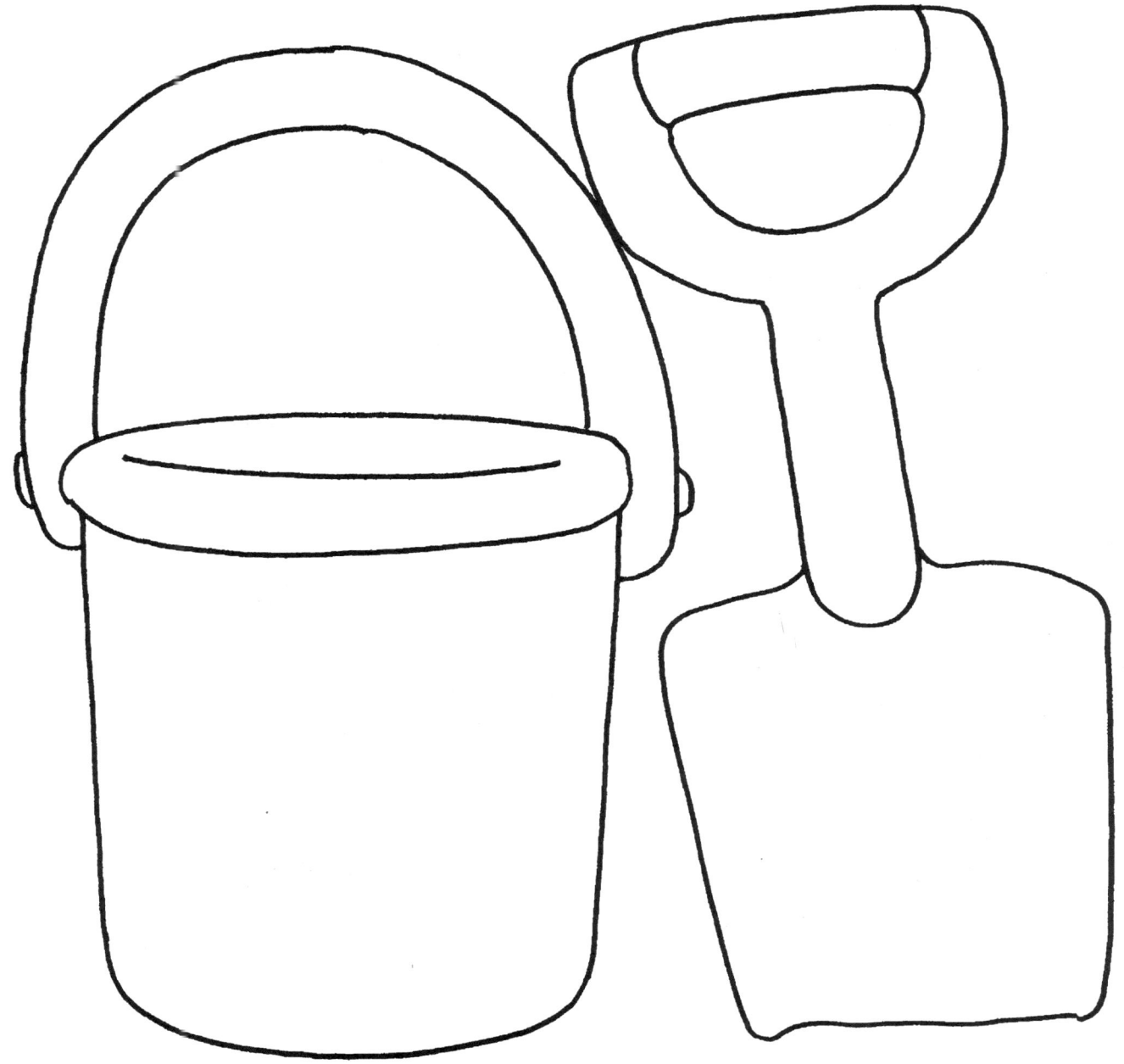

▲ EARLY YEARS ESSENTIALS FOR SCIENCE: Materials

Made from wood

You will need: a variety of wooden materials (ice lolly sticks, wood shavings, sawdust, matchsticks, offcuts), glue.

Use the materials to cover the wooden things below.

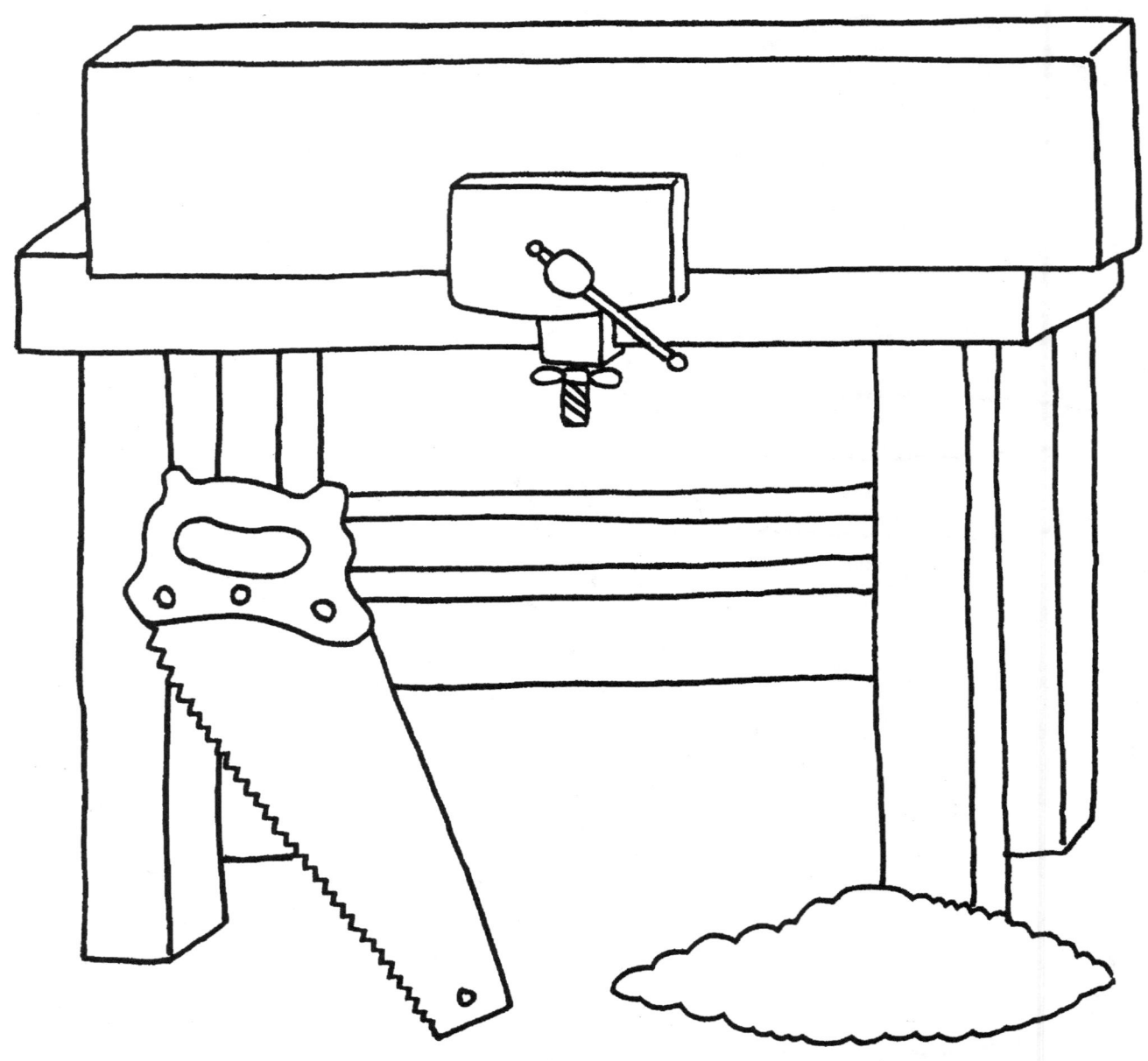

▲ Name _____

Made from metal

You will need: a variety of small metal objects (paper-clips, washers, bottle tops, scraps of foil and so on).

Use the objects to cover the metal parts of the van.

▲ EARLY YEARS ESSENTIALS FOR SCIENCE: Materials

▲ Name _____

Made from paper

You will need: tissue-paper, shiny coloured paper, wrapping paper, wallpaper, glue, scissors.

Choose a nice paper to cover the parcel.

▲ Name _____

Sort out the cupboard

You will need: a selection of dried pasta, pulses and similar foods, glue.

Sort the food into sets and fill up the shelves.

▲ Name _____

Magnetic materials

You will need: a selection of small objects (paper-clips, cotton reels, buttons, keys, paper-fasteners, coins, and so on).

Stick the objects the magnet picks up on to the drawing of a magnet below.

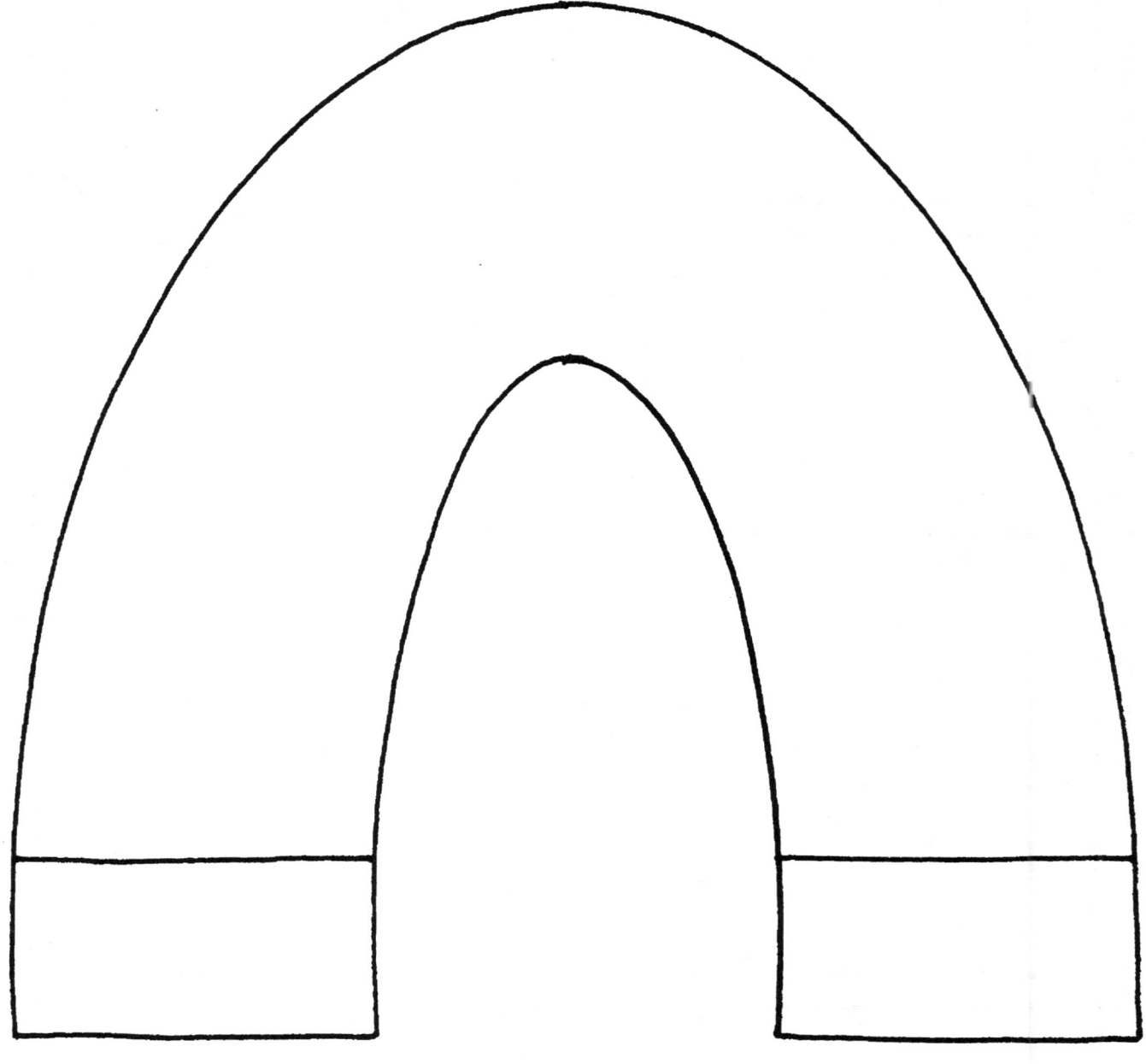

▲ EARLY YEARS ESSENTIALS FOR SCIENCE: Materials

▲ Name _____

Gone fishing

You will need: a set of fish, a fishing rod with a magnet, paper clips, a sheet for each player, crayons.

Who can catch the most fish?

▲ Name _____

Put them to bed

You will need: squares of different-coloured fabrics, glue, scissors.

Use the fabric pieces to make a patchwork quilt for the seven dwarfs.

▲ EARLY YEARS ESSENTIALS FOR SCIENCE: Materials

▲ Name _____

The lighthouse

You will need: a shiny or transparent material, red and white paper or fabric, matchsticks, blue and green tissue-paper, glue, scissors.

Use the materials to decorate the picture.

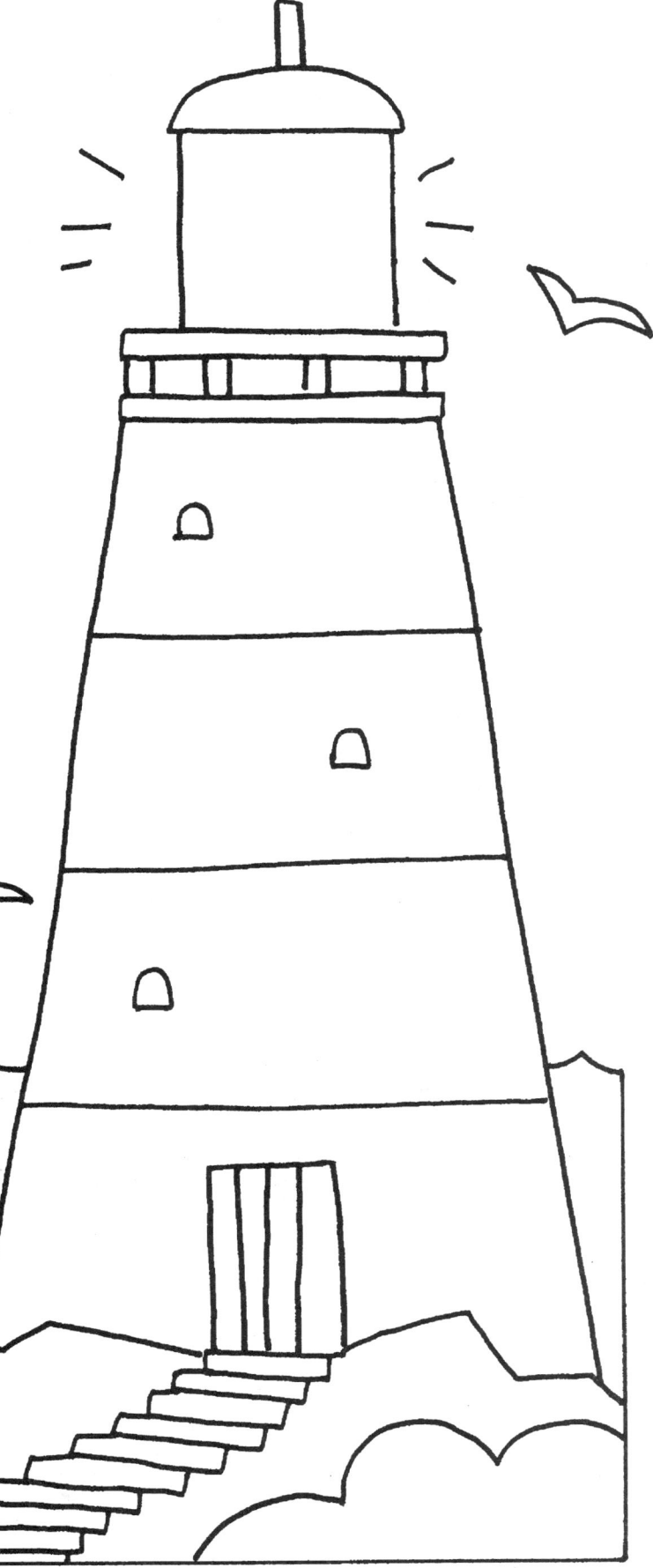

▲ EARLY YEARS ESSENTIALS FOR SCIENCE: Materials

▲ Name _____

Keeping dry

You will need: a variety of materials (plastic sheet, cotton fabric, paper, woollen material and lace), glue, scissors.

Which material is best for Teddy's umbrella? Stick it on to the picture.

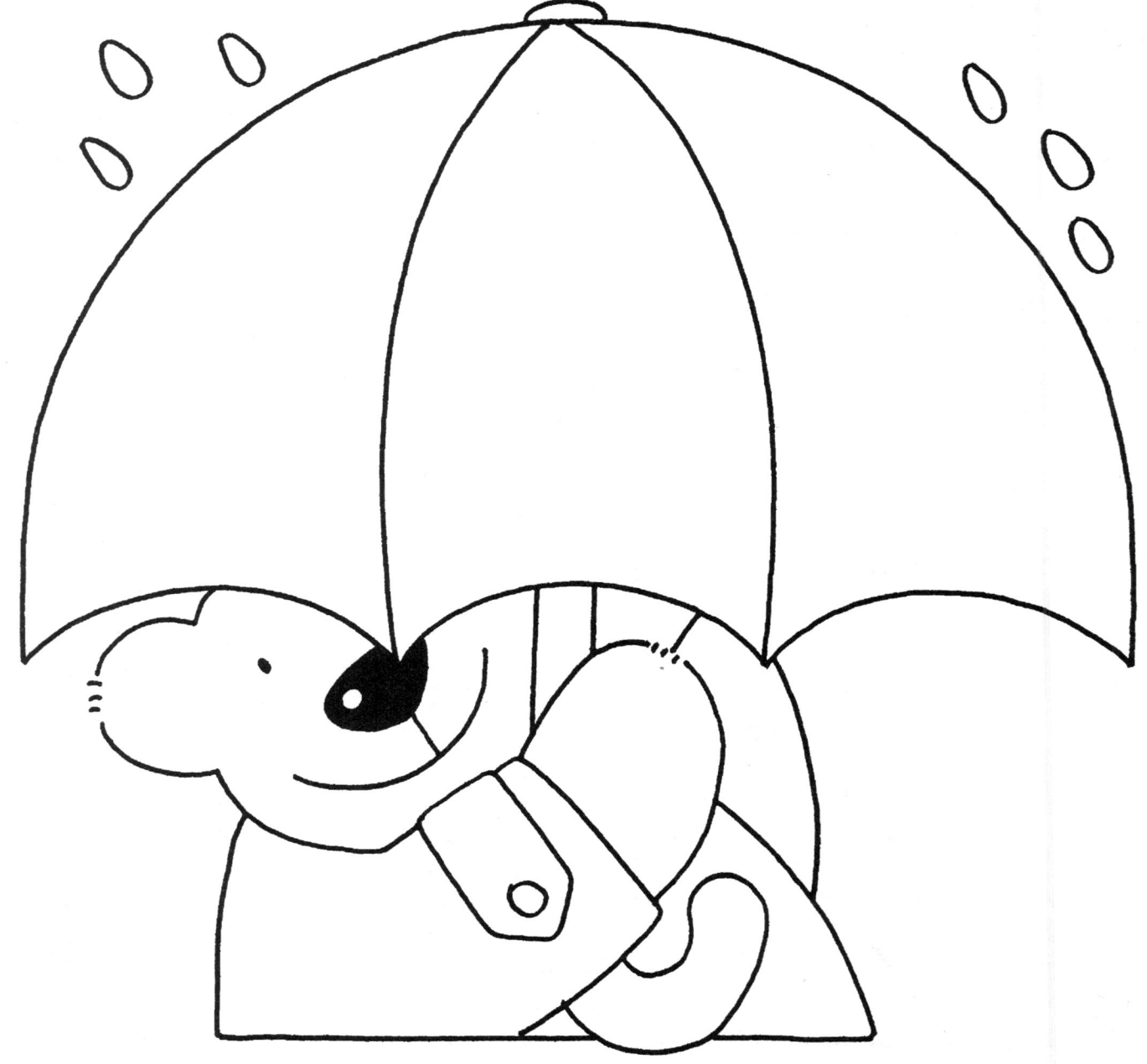

▲ EARLY YEARS ESSENTIALS FOR SCIENCE: Materials

▲ Name _____

See through it

You will need: various types of paper and materials (some transparent), scissors, glue.

Use a see-through material to cover the glass in the window.

▲ EARLY YEARS ESSENTIALS FOR SCIENCE: Materials

▲ Name _____

Keeping warm

You will need: a variety of woven and knitted woollen fabrics, thin cotton fabric, lace, plastic, glue, scissors.

Use the warmest fabrics to cover the clothes.
What material will you use for the boots?

▲ EARLY YEARS ESSENTIALS FOR SCIENCE: Materials

Keeping cool

You will need: cotton fabric, T-shirt material, fur fabric, woollen material, glue, scissors.

Use the coolest fabric to cover the clothes. What material will you use to cover Teddy?

The three little pigs

▲ Name _____

You will need: matchsticks, raffia, brick-shaped pieces of card, scissors, glue.

Use the materials to make three houses for the pigs.

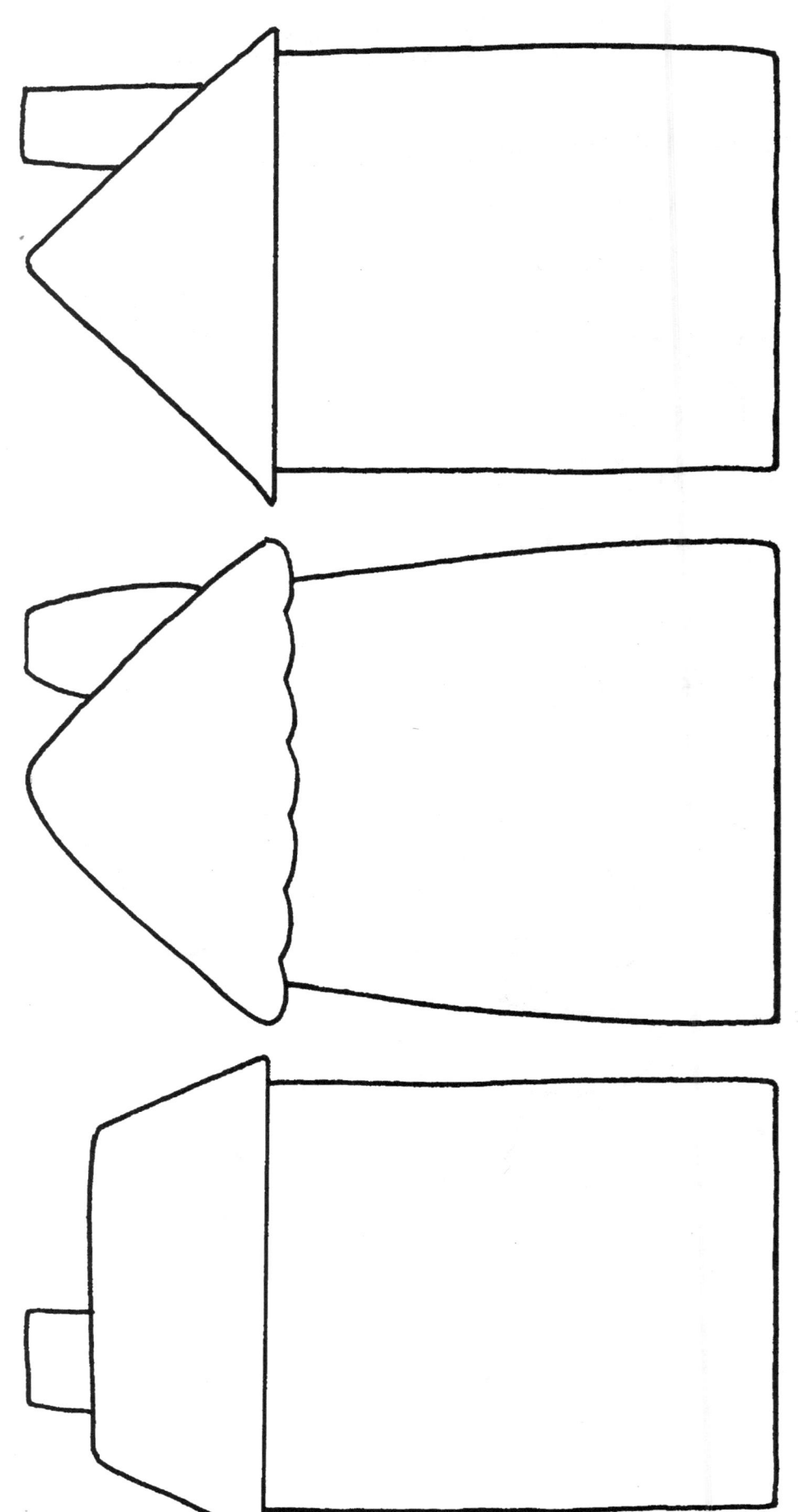

▲ EARLY YEARS ESSENTIALS FOR SCIENCE: Materials

▲ Name _____

Squashy things

You will need: the objects shown below, crayons.

Colour the things you can squeeze and squash.

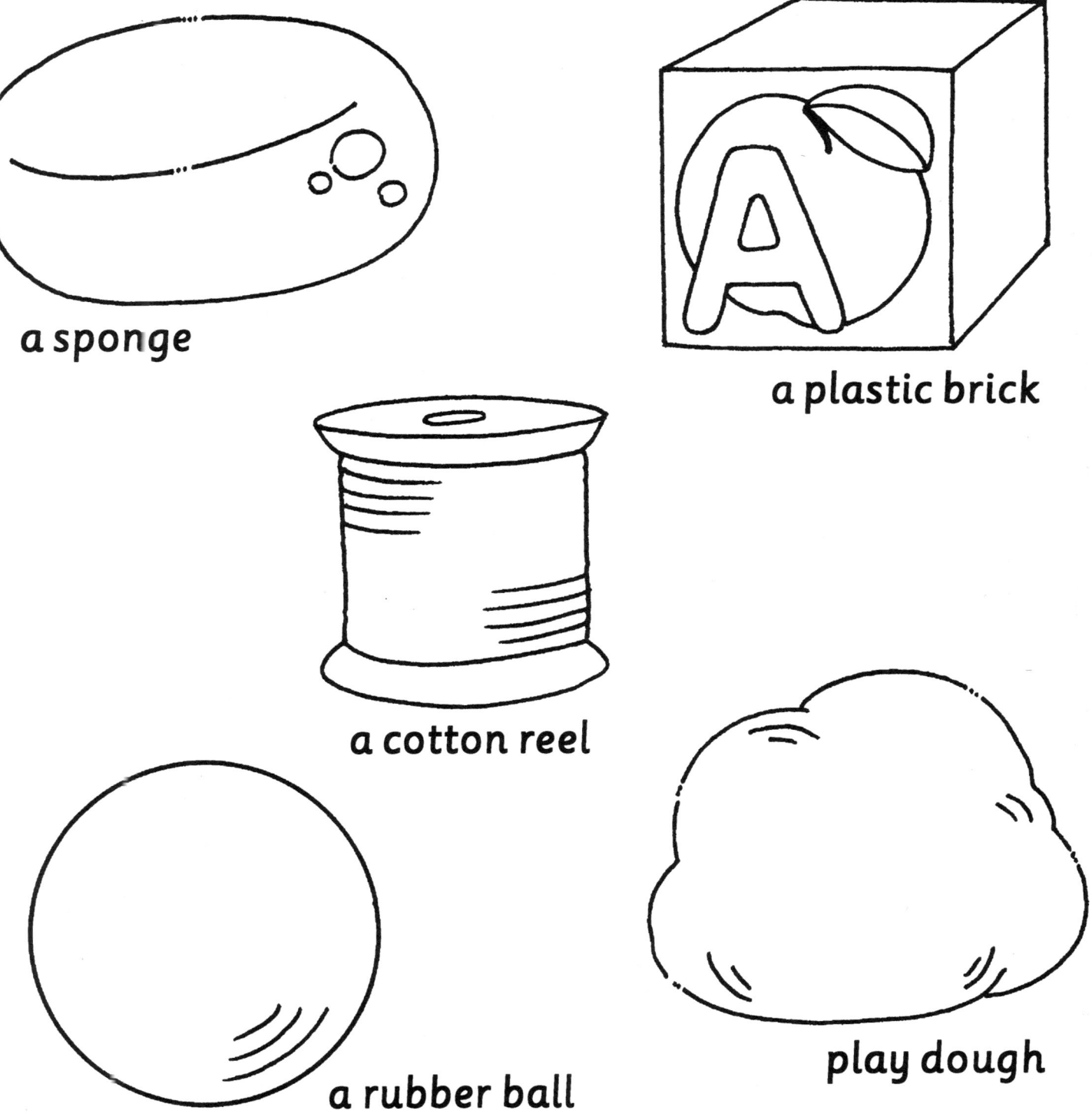

a sponge

a plastic brick

a cotton reel

a rubber ball

play dough

▲ EARLY YEARS ESSENTIALS FOR SCIENCE: Materials

▲ Name _____

Does it float?

You will need: a tank of water, a variety of small objects (a pencil, a coin, a cotton reel, a pebble, a lolly stick, a cork, a paper-clip), glue.

Do the objects float or sink? Stick them in the correct place on the drawing below.

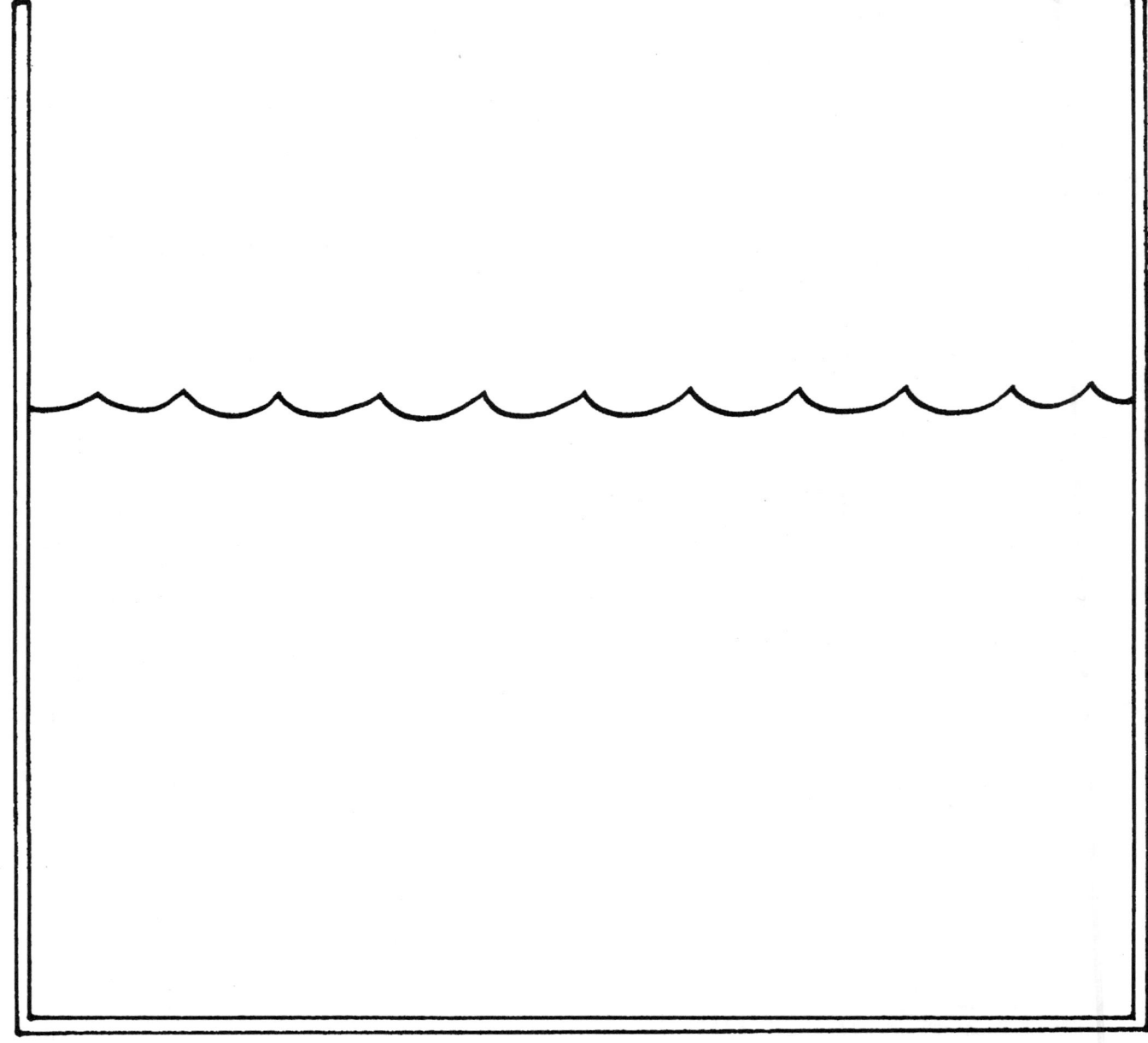

▲ Name _____

Can you wiggle it?

You will need: a range of flexible and inflexible materials, buttons or sequins, glue, scissors.

Use a wiggly material to make your snakes.
Give each snake a shiny eye.

▲ Name _____

Play dough shapes

You will need: play dough, a rolling pin.

Make these shapes from your play dough.

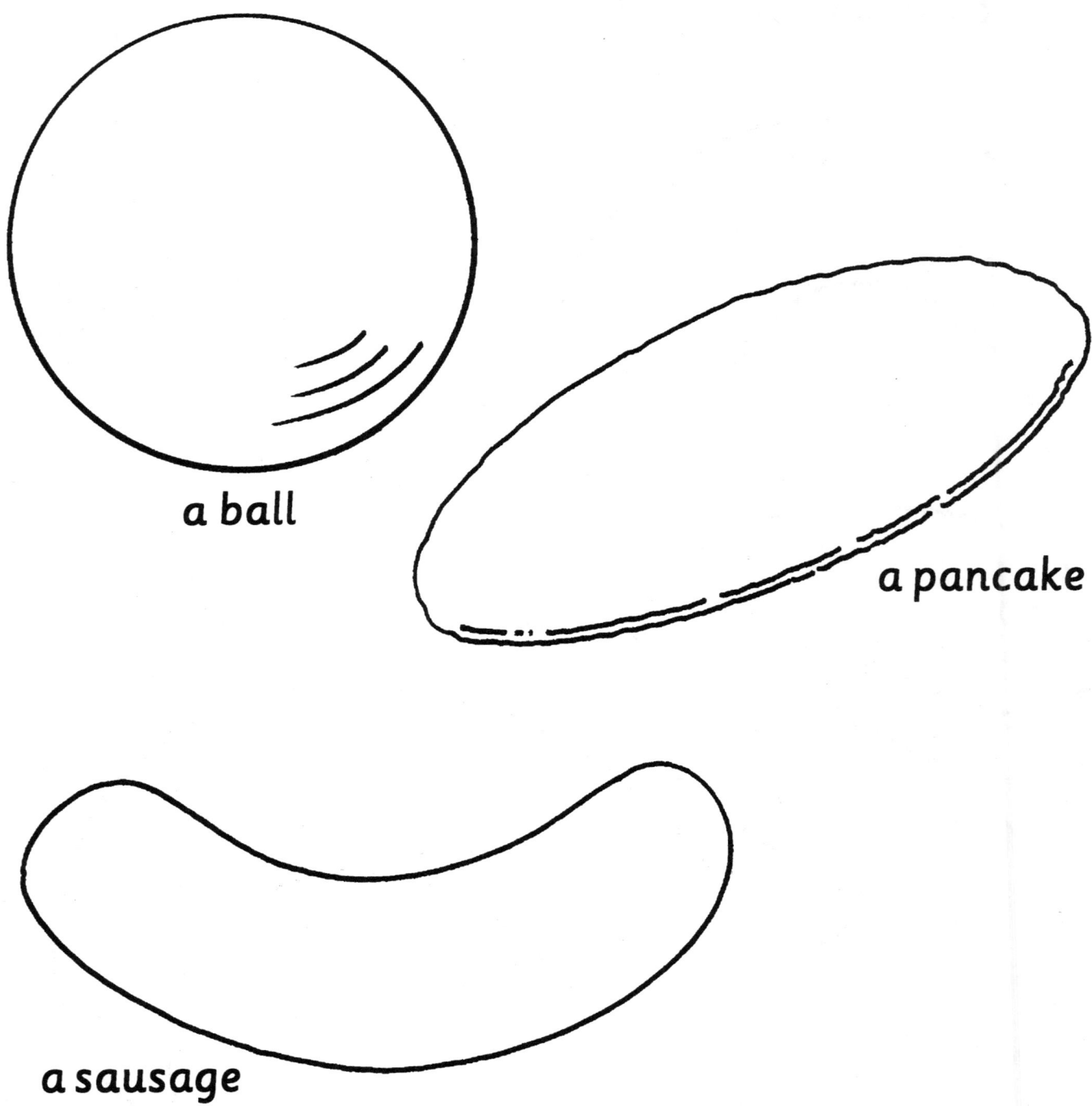

a ball

a pancake

a sausage

▲ EARLY YEARS ESSENTIALS FOR SCIENCE: Materials

▲ Name _____

Is it shiny?

You will need: shiny and dull materials cut into small pieces, glue.

Stick the shiny things on to the drawing to make a pretend mirror.

▲ Name _____

Make a snack mat

You will need: strips of coloured paper, glue.

Weave the paper in and out of the cut strips to make a pattern.

▲ EARLY YEARS ESSENTIALS FOR SCIENCE: Materials

▲ Name _____

Magic painting

You will need: wax crayons, very thin paint or ink, a paintbrush.

Colour the picture using the crayons. (Do not colour the sky.) Paint all over the picture.

▲ EARLY YEARS ESSENTIALS FOR SCIENCE: Materials

▲ Name _____

Sticky stuff

You will need: *pieces of fabric, paper, small pebbles, paper-clips, pasta, PVA glue, water paste.*

Try to stick the items into the spaces on this sheet.

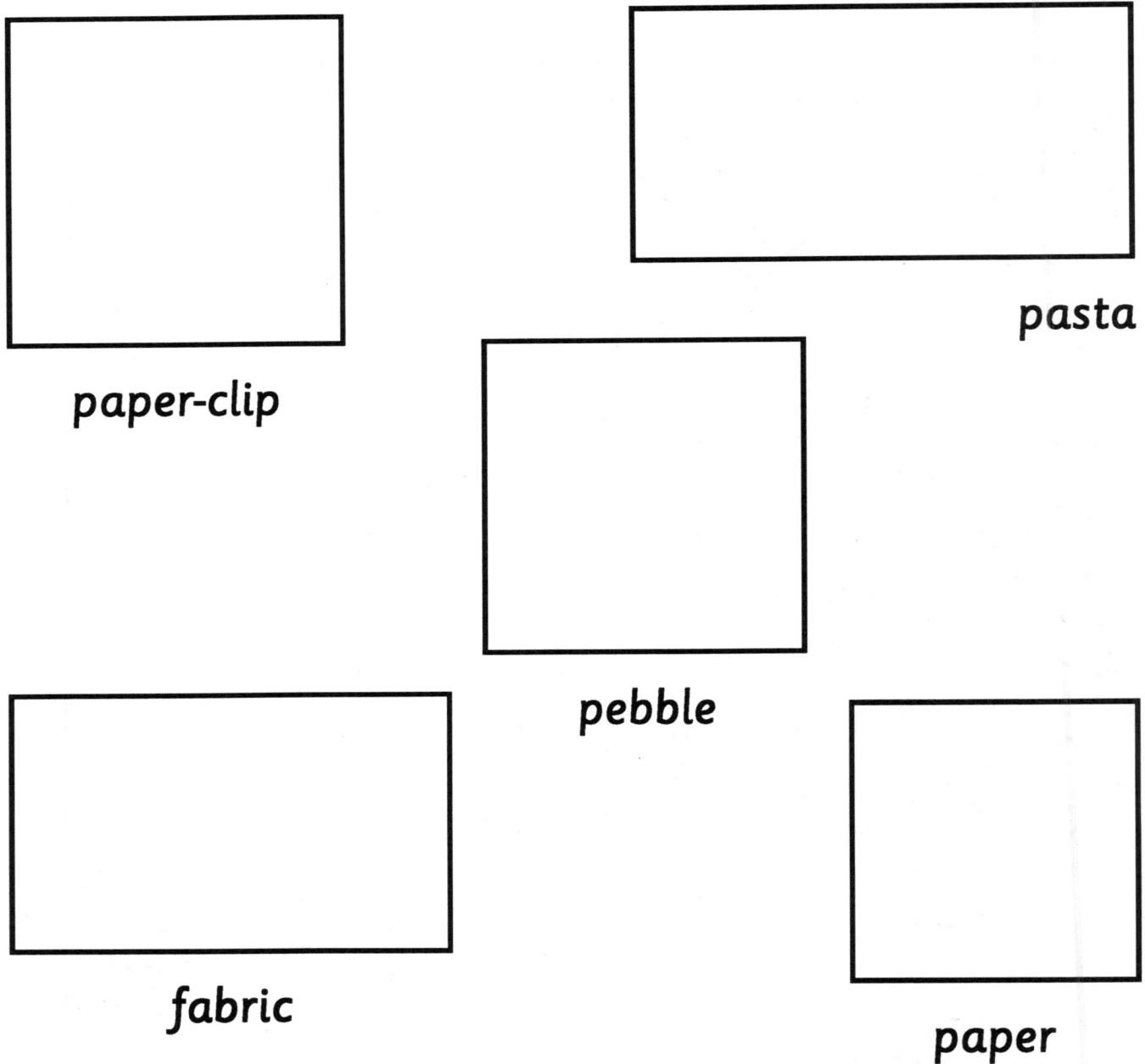

paper-clip

pasta

pebble

fabric

paper

Hold up the sheet to test the glue. Has it worked?

▲ EARLY YEARS ESSENTIALS FOR SCIENCE: Materials

▲ Name _____

Melting

You will need: crayons, scissors.

Match the pictures to show what the objects on the top row will look like when they have melted.

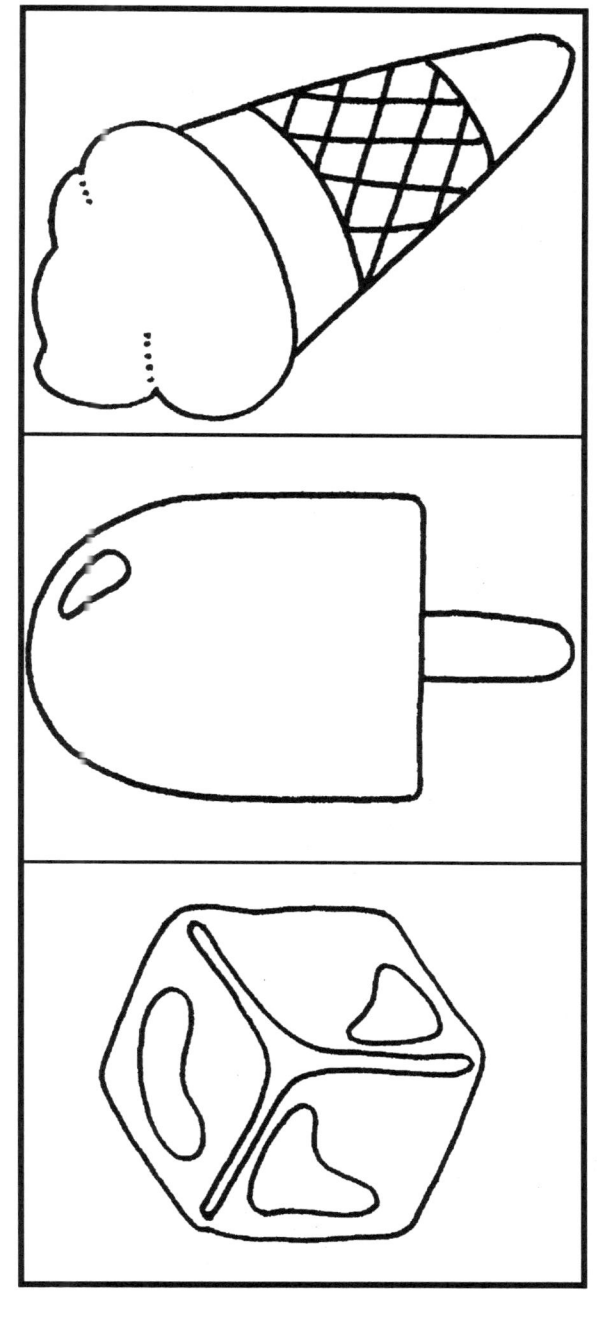
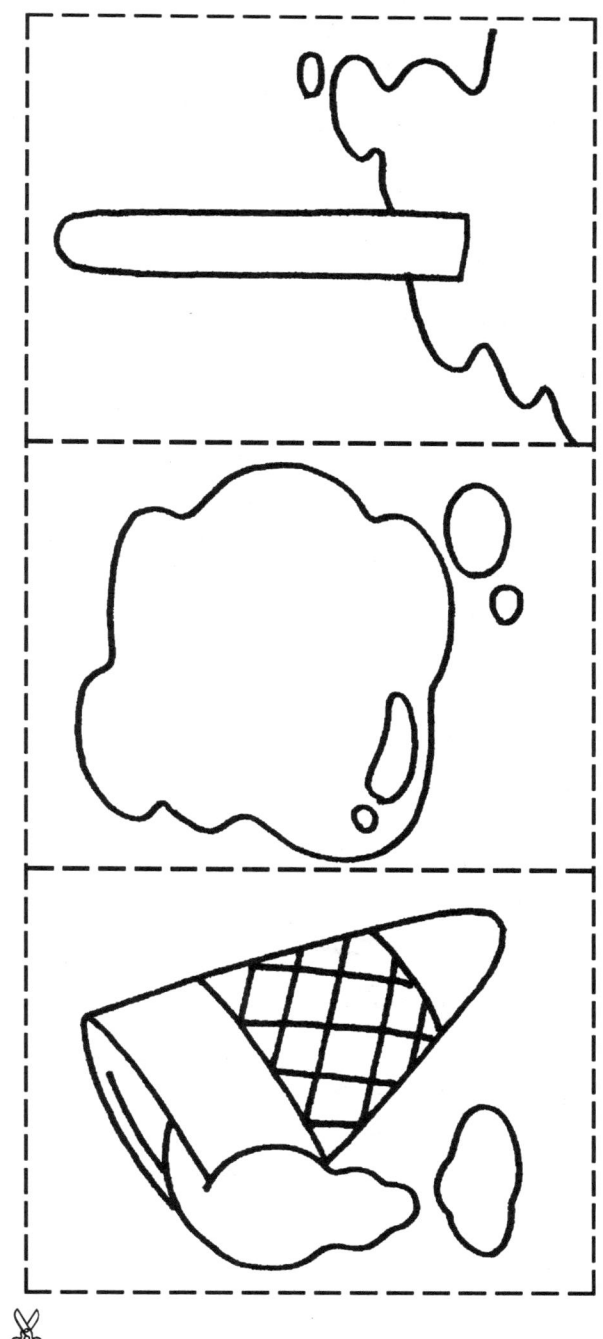

▲ Name _____

Lemonade

You will need: sherbet powder, a plastic glass, water, a spoon, crayons, small silver foil circles, glue.

Fill the glass with water, then add the sherbet powder and stir. What happens to the powder?
Now colour the drawing and add silver bubbles.

▲ EARLY YEARS ESSENTIALS FOR SCIENCE: Materials

▲ Name _____

Shades

You will need: paint, water, a yoghurt pot, a paintbrush, a plastic dropper or syringe.

Follow the instructions to colour in the snake.

I started with this colour.

I added one squirt of water.

I added two squirts.

I added three squirts.

I added four squirts.

I added five squirts.

▲ EARLY YEARS ESSENTIALS FOR SCIENCE: Materials

▲ Name _____

Blowing bubbles

You will need: bubble mixture, three bubble blowers in different shapes, a pencil.

Use the three bubble blowers to blow bubbles. What shape bubbles did you blow? Draw them.

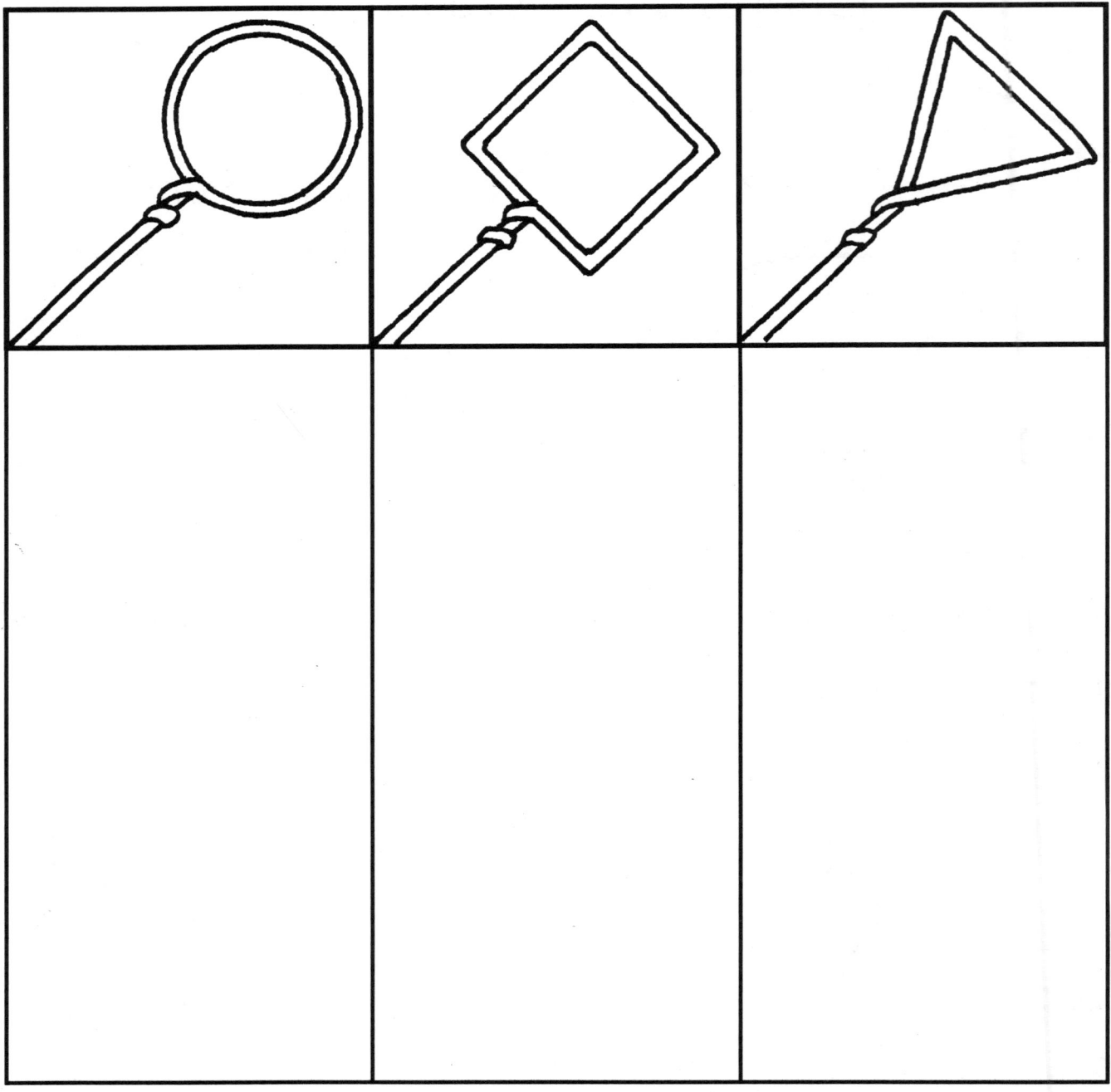

▲ EARLY YEARS ESSENTIALS FOR SCIENCE: Materials

▲ Name _____

Painting with soils

You will need: a range of different soils, paintbrushes, water.

Use the soils to paint the picture.

▲ EARLY YEARS ESSENTIALS FOR SCIENCE: Materials

▲ Name _____

Make a feely picture

You will need: a variety of materials (cotton, wool, sawdust, coconut fibre, matchsticks, foil paper, fine gravel, sand), PVA glue, scissors.

Use the materials to decorate the picture.

▲ Name _____

Sorting muesli

You will need: three different sieves (coarse, medium, fine), muesli, three bowls, sticky-backed plastic, scissors.

Sieve the muesli and stick down the pieces caught.

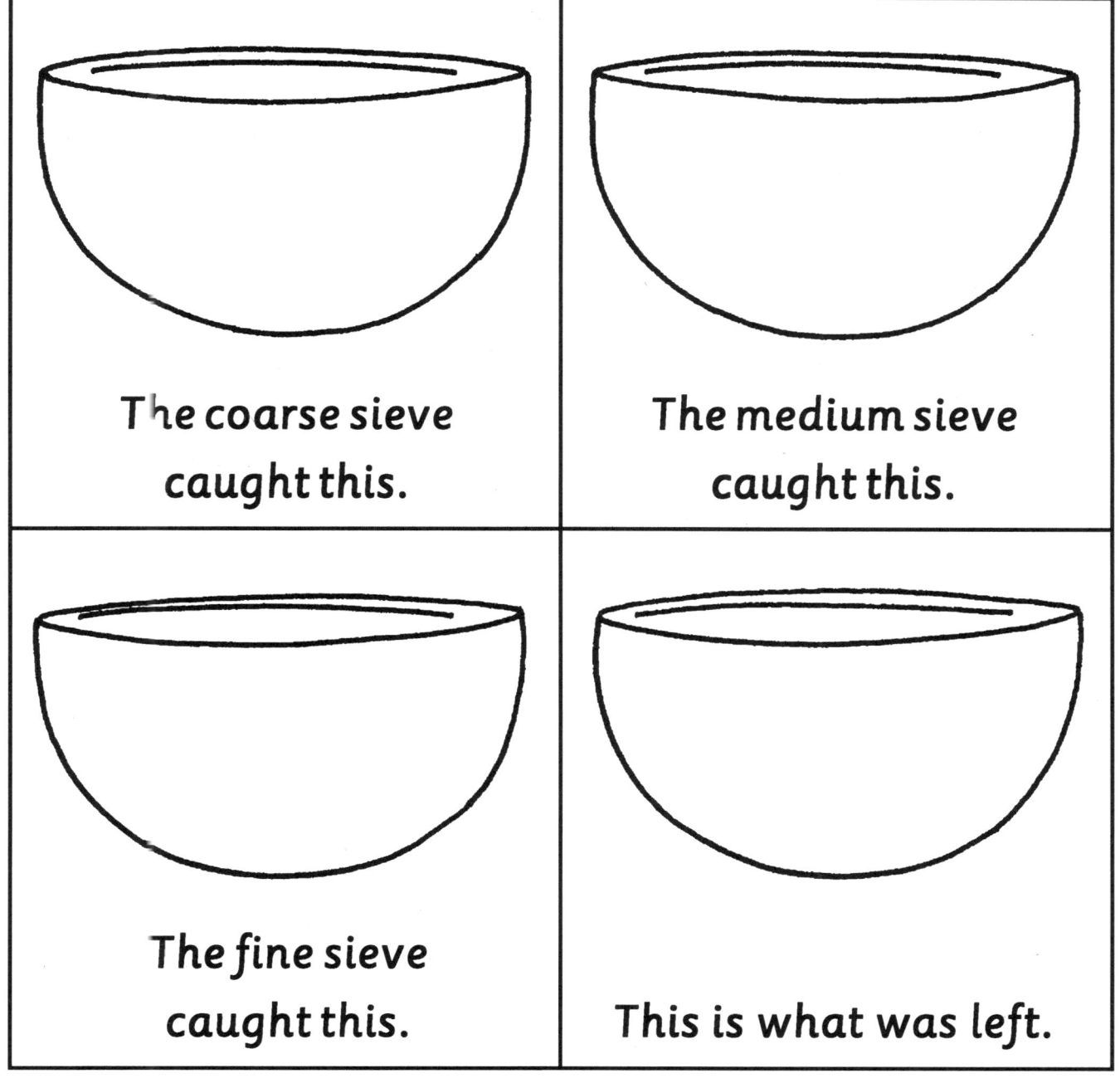

The coarse sieve caught this.

The medium sieve caught this.

The fine sieve caught this.

This is what was left.

▲ EARLY YEARS ESSENTIALS FOR SCIENCE: Materials

▲ Name _____

Texture dominoes

You will need: thick card, a selection of the materials listed on the cards below, scissors, glue.

fur fabric	foil	foil	knitted fabric
knitted fabric	fine sandpaper	fine sandpaper	a coil of string
a coil of string	paper	paper	velvet
velvet	coarse sandpaper	coarse sandpaper	corrugated card
corrugated card	string stripes	string stripes	plastic
plastic	canvas	fur fabric	fur fabric